GET UP ARISE

Boost your sales success

WORKSHOP IN A BOOK

RAJEEV NARANG

notionpress
.com

INDIA · SINGAPORE · MALAYSIA

Notion Press

No. 8, 3rd Cross Street,
CIT Colony, Mylapore,
Chennai, Tamil Nadu – 600 004

First Published by Notion Press 2021
Copyright © Rajeev Narang 2021
All Rights Reserved.

ISBN 978-1-63806-641-5

Dedicated to all Salespersons

With blessings of my Maa

Contents

Broadly the book has six chapters with loads of activities, exercises and bonus content inside each chapter. Take a quick peep into what this workbook has to offer.

The Context Building
The Key Challenges in Sales

Make a Sales Plan
The BANT Methodology
Segregating the Leads
Making Success Dashboard

Always Be Prepared
Making a Checklist

About the Author

Rajeev Narang is a Sales & Marketing Consultant and in his career spanning three decades has helped building many brands in diversified industries and has mentored, trained, and inspired thousands of sales persons.

Through this workbook he is sharing his experience of all these years, and the knowledge that he has gained while working with Promoters, Directors, CEOs, his Mentors and all the teams in small and big companies. Despite his immense experience, Rajeev still considers himself as a learner and emphasizes on the fact that the word "LEARNING" includes "EARNING" and therefore imbibes the same thought among his mentees, circle and teams.

He has positioned himself has the Possibility of Creativity & Contribution and he believes in giving back to the world by way of sharing what he has got. He is on a mission to upgrade the skills of people working in the domain of sales & marketing through workshops, training, guest lectures in educational institutes and companies.

He is a TEDx Speaker, a Laughter Ambassador, conducts stress management workshops, founded a social project – Phenk Mat, an anti-car litter program.

Insights and Praises for the Book

This book contains a complete package of Sales team training, motivation filled with engagement, as it's based on identifying the gaps in selling process, completing the loop from lead generation to acquisition thus enhancing the productivity which is really worth reading & practicing.

The 6 chapters are like a real Work book as per the content being included in it, which will certainly help to practice it to gain success & keep succeeding in sales segment.

I wish a great success to all the professionals, which will certainly make one as to GET UP & ARiSE!!

Pramod Kumar Rajput
Sr Vice President & Vertical Head
Cadila Pharmaceutical Limited

The preeminent thing in the book is that it simplifies the steps to boost the performance. Personally knowing Rajeev, it is most important to understand that all in this book says comes with his lifetime work experience towards sales and marketing. He has always been a great speaker and motivator and I am sure this book will help many in contravention the blocks to ascent the prodigious mountain of success. A great book and must read.

Aseem Kumar Singh
Vice President – Sales
AIPL Zorro Pvt. Ltd.

As a sales enthusiast, what arrests my attention is "It's a Workbook and not a Book" I must say quite impressive. This Workbook is practical in it's approach and guides a learner through sequential activities to experience the problems in hand. It resonates with a typical sales person's day and let's him deep dive into a situation to bring in the elixir of life. The author has touched upon beautifully how Sales is a low-pressure task creating a pull if the customers are understood and decoded right. Each chapter unfolds an interesting story of every sales individual. Sneaking in for the right buying signals is an interesting pick. The science and art of selling are well poised.

A holy grail indeed!

Ruchi Shah Bhogra
Associate Director, Career Management Services,
School of Inspired Leadership

I am a Sales Director and I deal with international markets, practically I am a salesman, yes because we all are salesmen in everyday life, and I have been doing it for thirty years now. That sounds like a long time, but the real salesman never stops learning, indeed he must continue to learn.

Precisely for this deep conviction of mine, years ago we decided with my colleagues in Delhi to look for an expert in communication and sales techniques.

To be honest we didn't know exactly who we were looking for, but we knew our salespeople needed to grow, to train.

It was then that I met Rajeev, and his communicative energy that can influence anyone. He was already taking care of our Brand's image, but he realized that our salesmen were like plants in a garden, and he had the vision and conviction of a gardener.

Yes, because a gardener puts order in the garden, gives it shape, he takes care of the suffering ones and makes the smaller plants grow, all with a precise design, all with a very specific project. And today our sales force (our wonderful garden) has really grown, and I can credit this to Rajeev.

This is Rajeev's strength, this is his meritorious work, and in the book, or rather the Worbook, he does exactly this: he lists, explains, illustrates and explores the contents of "every seller's toolbox". Rajeev helps plants to strengthen themselves, to grow, to reach their maximum splendour, in a continuous updating to the market context.

Rajeev helps us to develop awareness of our path.

A useful book for sellers or future sellers, that I will take it with me on my next trips, to consult it every now and then. And I think will be very often!

Ugo Pelosin
Export Director,
Wood Coatings Export Sales Dept,
Sirca S.p.A., Italy

GET UP; ARiSE is inspiring workbook especially about the Live Workshops that lifted me up as a Sales Leader.

It demonstrates the important sales principle through simple communication technique Rajeev has discerned from working, training and mentoring more than thousands of sales and marketing professionals. Indeed a workbook handy for all sales professionals with or without sales training to understand the very importance of sales training and practice in our day to day life where Everyday Counts. Not just this, but He has also highlighted most important concern of the Organizations " the importance of investment into Sales training and the role of trained sales infrastructure in the success of any Organization as ' Sales is like a muscle that needs to be exercised Everyday in order to grow stronger'.

'This Workbook amazingly comes from Live workshop poured into six particularly powerful chapters demonstrates and shares creative ways for the growth of sales professionals and Organization. Prayers and best wishes for this sincere efforts by Rajeev ji to reach out to Readers Sales Heroes - The Real Heroes of the Organization'.

Shekhar Khanna
Sales Leader and Sr. General Manager - Sales
Hindustan Pencils Limited

Completely floored by this exciting step-by-step guide to become a great sales person. The "workbook" has some valuable and practical insights written in a simple manner. Rajeev has beautifully captured some hard-hitting truths that we often tend to ignore. A must read for all who want to make it big in their selling career.

Anshu G. Bhogra
Head – Planning, Buying & Ecommerce
Forever New

Workshop in a book sounds wonderful and amazing. The book is a comprehensive anthology of the Art, Science and often ignored Psychology of sales and an answer to those who say selling cannot be taught.

The book is step-by-step breakdown of the sales process and seeks to demystify and debunk some common myths and misconceptions. It takes a systemic approach and if followed diligently and with discipline, this can help sales turnaround no doubt.

Having seen Rajeev in action for over 15 years and as an active participant in a few of the workshops I have no doubts about the effectiveness of the content. I wish everyone who is reading to GET SET GROW! And all the best to future Sales Rock Stars!

Ira Sahai
Marketing Consultant

GET UP ARiSE is a compendium of practical tips for salesperson in any sector. Salesmanship is both a scientific and a creative process; and is based on deep understanding of human psychology and a generous dollop of common sense!

Anybody who meticulously follows the book will surely elevate his skills to stratospheric heights!! The insights herein are distilled from a lifetime of Rajeev›s experience as hands-on sales professional and a marketing guru and mentor.

His next level workshops have helped innumerable salesmen and business leaders alike. This book brilliantly captures all of it. For best results, this book should be used as a workbook

I recommend the book to people in domains other than direct selling as well; these insights are relevant to all professionals and at all levels.

Sudhanshu Srivastava
Product Management Lead
Bharat Insecticides Ltd
A group company of Mitsui and Co.

Sales is one of the most challenging careers one can choose. It gives you an opportunity to network with a plethora of interesting persons & organizations.

Experienced professionals like Rajeev Narang can teach nuances of sales in the easiest possible manner.

The Workshop Technique is simply superb, as it not only covers the essentials but also gives you an up-close view of the market realities. Deep insights into sales terminologies and connecting them to everyday situations has been done superbly... Learning's come with examples that are easily relatable to salespersons everyday situations.

Overall it's a remarkable effort that focuses on developing the right attitude required in sales coupled with a systematic approach towards honing your sales skills in a meticulous manner..

This book will be the best asset for every salesperson who wishes to excel and become a business leader...

Vivek Nanda
Corporate Leader/Sales Veteran/Visiting Professor

"THIS BOOK MAKES YOU SALE-ABLE"

We are always selling. And this book makes you SALES READY. Winning an opinion is also winning a sales pitch.

The objection handling techniques have helped me a lot in real business scenarios. Before reading this, I thought I knew the game, but it's altogether an exponential version of things. A technique from this book that I use on a daily basis: *"when you want the prospect to make a decision, offer him two options. He will always choose one".* Hoping to see this book in a digital format like an interactive app.

Rahul Gauba
CEO, The Saint

"Great things are done by a series of small things done together".

This workbook reminds me of the above quote. Perfect blend of knowing what to do, how to do and when to do to achieve desired results. I recommend all the readers who want to make their career in sales should read this piece of work, which is a perfect combination of subjective and objective approach.

Congratulations Mr. Rajeev Narang on writing such a Gem of work.

Himanshu Issar
GM - Sales & Marketing
Ajit Industries Pvt. Ltd.

GET UP ARiSE is a workbook, which provides an individual and an organization with lot of tools and tips on how one can boost sales. The content of workbook is very simple and easy to follow; we just need to do one thing - PRACTICE.

I am among few lucky ones who attended this workshop twice – once alone and another time with my team. Believe me both the times I learned something new and whenever we have some challenges in our organization we just go back to our notes.

I am very glad and like to congratulate Rajeevji for converting the workshop into a workbook and making his valuable knowledge, experience and insights available to mass audience. I personally believe that this workshop, now a workbook can add lots of value and direction in every organization's sales training program and help in boosting the Sales.

All the chapters covered in the workbook are very helpful in sales training. I personally benefited from some tools like - The 20x4 rule, Being FABulous and Retention.

If you are reading this that means you have manifested for this and the investment that you have made on this workbook will give you multiple fold returns. But please use it as a WORKBOOK and not read it as any other business book.

Yogesh Mittal
Managing Director,
Elite String Apparel Pvt. Ltd.

"This book is a masterpiece to become a sales master!"

'Sales' is an integral part of any business you are in and this book is full of insights, practical strategies that work in real life to help you improvise your sales.

Rajeev Narang sir has shared his treasure of knowledge from his life's precious experience and sales mastery. It is coming from a man who has walked the talk and 'Get up ARiSE' is sure shot success book to inspire you for high-class performance generating lofty sales for the organization.

The book reiterates and teaches you some of the key aspects like sales is not about selling as it is about finding the trust using the right tactics and educating your clients for a mutual winning move.

I have witnessed Rajeev sir delivering consistently to his attendees, clients with super value workshops. His stage presence, power of smile, high energy, and value creation is majestic and he makes sales sound so simple, appealing and attractive with his ability to share 21st century modalities and ideology.

Rajeev sir is the real possibility of creativity and contribution and this book is awe-inspiring work based on the real solutions to build profitable business through sales.

Get ready to change your story in sales.

Author Sherry
International Public Speaking Coach and
recognized by many as #1 in India.
(Global Conference Speaker, 7 times Intl.
TEDx Speaker, 3 times Josh Talks Speaker,
Author of Intl. Best Sellers)
Founder, President & Organizer MS Talks™ India
MD, CEO Public Speaking Institute™

Foreword

It is indeed gratifying and exhilarating to write the foreword for this book in a world that is full of books and literature on achieving Sales Success. What makes this book DIFFERENT from others is that it is not a book full of '*Gyaan*' but takes a refreshing and innovative approach of being - a Workshop in a book. This makes it highly practical, easy to understand, and doable by anyone in the sales profession, who wants to succeed in a challenging, demanding, and complex world of Sales.

Rajeev has over two decades of quality experience in sales management in various prestigious organizations. He has also been an extremely respected and accomplished trainer and consultant, who has not only been successful in bringing out the essence of sustainable sales practices but also presented it in a way which each one of us can identify with and capture **nuances** of the complete selling process. This is an outcome of personally training thousands of sales professionals in various corporates in the last many years, across diverse industries.

I have known Rajeev for over 2 decades & having known him personally & professionally, I feel he is the person who could have written such book, which comes with rare insights into the minds of not only the buyer but salesperson as well & putting it together in his inimitable style.

He walks the talk & time and again, he REINVENTED himself, from being a corporate executive to Sales & Marketing Consultant, founded Aarogyalay, positively impacting the minds of thousands as TEDx speaker and discharging his duty as a responsible citizen by his social initiatives under Phenk Mat program. To me Rajeev demonstrates what it takes to keep adding value to not his students but society at large through his many avtars.

We all have been witnessing the Covid-19 pandemic, the unprecedented times, something that has had far-reaching consequences in every sphere of human life. This event for sure is going to help us understand the importance of agility, adaptability, and the value of relationships. The time has come to press the **ReSet** button to make changes in our daily lives, at least at a pace, we can comfortably commit to. The title of the book " GET UP ARiSE" is quite apt for the current and the coming times.

It is not easy being a sales professional, a world full of immense opportunities and challenges. With due respect to all the functions in an organization, we all know, sales is the life-blood and the most important role in every business. Sales professionals have obligation to generate revenue for the organization, and thus they are under constant pressure to WIN so that organizations can be successful and continue to grow.

Unfortunately, most of the organizations do not INVEST enough to upskill the sales team members to make the sales team more productive, improve sales win ratios, improve soft skills, etc. There is a compelling need to impart sales teams the " Know Hows " of high-performance selling than leaving to them the " Some Hows " to get the sales for the organization. This is where I personally feel this book will be a great resource and a much-needed tool for any sales professional, irrespective of the industry.

In the sales profession, the sky is the only limit for growth. This is extremely rewarding and fulfilling, but at times can be stressful too, as pressure is always on you to improve your performance month on month. Thus to be a Sales Champ, you have to believe in yourself, when nobody else will. You have to be self-motivated and have an insatiable desire, which will be the key to your success. Success belongs to those who are well prepared to grab the opportunities as and when they present themselves. Remember, there is no short cut to success. Positive attitude, hard work, and the desire to be the very best can take you miles ahead.

You are the CEOs of your life, be prepared to take ownership of the outcomes, instead of holding external events or others responsible for your success as well as failures. Let me quote legendary Jack Welch, "Control your destiny or someone else will". A successful person is always willing to learn from failures and use it as a tool to improve oneself.

I sincerely hope that " Get UP ARiSE " will inspire all the readers to become the best version of themselves and dream big. Get UP ARiSE!

Sanjay Tiwari
Sales Veteran & Corporate Leader

Preface

Unbelievable! But true. It is finally happening, this book is finally being published. I am amazed at myself and at this wonderful process of book writing.

It has taken me more than two years to complete this piece of my heart and soul (with a lot of effort done by my brain) and finally I see my first ever baby taking shape. If you are wondering what took me so long, you will know once you read it.

If you have noticed the cover of the book, it reads Workshop in a book! Yes, you read it right, it is a workshop "Boost Your Sales Success" which has been converted into a book. That is the reason I prefer to call it a Workbook.

When I started my journey as a Sales & Marketing Consultant in 2001, most of my clients were small & medium enterprises who wanted my assistance in becoming organized companies with a recognized brand. None of them was a start-up; everyone had reached a particular level of turnover, profitability, and operations. But their need to have recognition as a brand and an organization was not fulfilled. That is when I came into the picture and gave them the desired impetus that satiated their hunger.

While every Brand that I worked with, belonged to a different industry, I noticed one common issue that each organization had. That was, Sales team's performance & productivity, which was considered as the only parameter for success. It was in their rights to expect their teams to perform and achieve the desired targets, but not a single company was investing on Sales Team training, motivation, and engagement. No wonder, not all the sales team members performed well and the attrition rate was high.

Throughout my entire career in dealing with Sales Teams, I have persuaded my customers to invest in Sales Team's motivation, training, and enabling them with the right tools. Therefore I took it upon myself to train the teams of my client organizations and ensured that they stay motivated and connected with the company. It didn't stop at training; rather it included incentive programs, sales meets, and rewards for extraordinary performers. This allowed me to enroll each one of the sales teams into the new reporting structures that I introduced in their companies.

The Sales Training that I gave to my clients' teams became more professional, and well formatted and were introduced as the "Sales Presentations that Sell" module in the year 2016. And then these modules evolved through the year and were then launched as Next level Future-ready Workshop "Boost Your Sales Success". After numerous workshops and helping thousands of salespeople, the workshop has come in form of this Workbook.

I hope this workbook enables you to achieve your desired success.

It is a must-read for all the salespersons, who have never attended any Sales Training program and their companies don't have that as a part of their agenda. It is easy –read with points and tips that you can use for ready reference while working in your area of business.

I encourage Sales Managers to use this book to train their teams as they work in the market. Upgrading the subordinates is a mark of true leadership, and that is how I see the Sales Managers as.

The readers should expect the following results after completion of this workbook:

- They will be able to identify the gaps in their selling process and they will get the tips to bridge those gaps
- They will know, how to look at the complete process of sales, from lead generation to acquisition, to the stage, when the customer becomes loyal and refers you to new prospects
- They should become pro at identifying buying signals from customers that will lead to increasing their productivity and therefore success

One last point, there was so much more that could have been added to this workbook. But I refrained from doing so as that would make it too much of a load at one point. If you find this workbook useful, do tell me; that will be my motivation to write the detailed version.

Happy reading, and happy selling.

Rajeev Narang

Acknowledgements

As I said this workbook is a slice from my 30years career out of which I have learnt being a Sales & Marketing Consultant for almost two decades. We all know that no journey is treaded alone. You always have many more people, who support you, guide you, push you and stand by you. These are the people who love and want only the best of you and therefore at many times be your hardest critics, teachers, and coaches.

Through this journey, I have been inspired and mentored by many great people and organizations. They include my clients, my associates, my team, my mentors and coaches, many like-minded personalities, and of course, my critics.

Here are some rock stars of my life, who have helped me shape my journey and this workbook.

My mother, who has been the superpower, and the biggest inspiration in my life. Thank you for your unconditional love and support in everything that I have chosen to do.

My Dad-in-law, the great Saini Saab, who held my hand at the most difficult times in my life and guided me in the right direction.

Late Mr. D. K. Jain, CMD of Luxor-Parker Group, taught me how to think big and how to share with the world, what you have.

Deepak Mehrotra Sir, for his guidance, inspiration, training, and mentoring during my early years in the career. A lot of this book has what you have taught me.

Vivek Govil, my first boss at Parker, who inspired me to be a great boss.

Ajit Gupta, who has been a client, friend, an inspiration, and a powerhouse of energy. Without his trust in me, it was not possible to create a brand like AIPL. Thank you for supporting my vision for Next Level Training Workshop.

Chanan Rohiwal, for believing in me and also teaching me to be business-like, over and above the friendships.

My special thanks to Author Sherry for inspiring me to adopt my workshop into a book, and Sanjay Tiwari for writing the Foreword with total belief.

My team members at Brand Buzz, who have always stood by me in all my endeavors and ridiculous demands for new and more ideas, every time. Guys, I am because you are.

Aayushi Vashishta for enhancing the value of the content of this book, Takshi Batra and Patricia Alexandar for putting it all together, Satnam Singh, for the various versions of the book cover, Yogesh Kashyap for the illustrations, and Kanchan Sharma for all the support during the workshops.

Last but surely not the least, the power girls in my life; Mamta, Anju, Meenu, Gunjan, and Akanksha, whom I look up to, every time I need energy, inspiration love and understanding. Without you all, my life does not move. Thank you for being there.

Thank you once again. I hope your love; blessings and efforts fulfill the dreams of the readers.

Rajeev Narang

Remember! It's Not a Book – It's a Workbook

The book flows like a live workshop, you keep going through the pages and practice through activities, exercises, just like a workshop. And as a result, you learn.

Make sure you don't jump the chapters.

The workbook will still be complete if you choose to skip the activities, but it is advisable that you complete the activities and exercises that are given during or after every chapter. Take notes, mark your clarifications, and mail them to me at workbook@rajeevnarang.in.

And before you start reading the workbook, I have a promise to make.

I am committed to your Sales Success and therefore will be available to answer your questions and clarifications from the book or from your work. Please write to me and should respond to you at the earliest possible time.

Get, Set, Grow.

GET UP, ARiSE

Your journey begins

Chapter ONE

Sales Successes (& Challenges)

SUCCESS – Google defines 'Success' as the accomplishment of an aim or purpose.

The word success could mean different things in different aspects. At one time, success could be attributed to the completion of an entire project, at the other time; success could be dependent upon a single component of a project.

Success could mean different attainments and accomplishments to different people. For one, it could be attaining a career goal, a personal home, a car, marital bliss, and for another it could mean leading a team or owning a business or achieving their targets month after month, to be always on the top.

This workbook is about Sales Success.

So let us understand, what ensures success in sales? Is it about achieving your (the sales person's) individual targets, or about achieving company targets? Does the success in sales reflect upon success in business?

In all my experiences as an entrepreneur, through many rounds of acquiring new customers, losing some of them to retaining few of them for years and years together, I have learned that we are successful as a salesperson, only if-

- We have a long-lasting relationship with our customers
- Our customers endorse and refer us to new prospects
- We are growing both vertically and horizontally

The first two points are dependent on how we acquire clients and how we manage them in the course of a continued relationship with them. The last point needs a deep understanding, as that is the most important aspect for getting growth in business.

Therefore the following two components of sales are very important, that facilitates one to determine sales success:

- HORIZONTAL GROWTH
- VERTICAL GROWTH

Horizontal growth pertains to expansion of customer base, while Vertical growth relates to working on the existing customer base, either by selling more of existing products/ services or by selling them new products/variants.

In one of the Next level workshops for Sales Persons in B2B space, one of the participants, Tushar, raised a concern that he was facing. He said that though he has achieved his targets every month, since last one year, he has not seen any substantial growth in total business, that doesn't make him extraordinary in the eyes of the sales manager, and he has never won the 'Salesman of the Quarter Award' that his company bestowed on the person who achieves the highest growth, over and above his or her target.

What do you think could be the reason?

Upon checking from him, I realized that though his number of customers and business thereof remained the same, he generally had a few of existing customers being replaced by some new clients. What do you think was going on?

Let me tell you, what it was. While Tushar was making a lot of effort in acquiring new customers, and he did, but he was not able to retain his existing customers. He was possibly not engaging them enough or was unable to give them more or newer solutions.

So if you have a range to sell, keep selling the existing products to existing customers, but also offer them new products so that you have better revenue from them. This is what we call Vertical growth as you go a little deep and intensive with the existing customers. You will be able to build a better relationship with the customer, with better value billing to him, a long relationship, and if you engage him well, you may have not only as a loyal customer but also as someone who could endorse you to his network.

This would be a perfect case to define Sales Success.

But does success come without challenges?

NEVER.

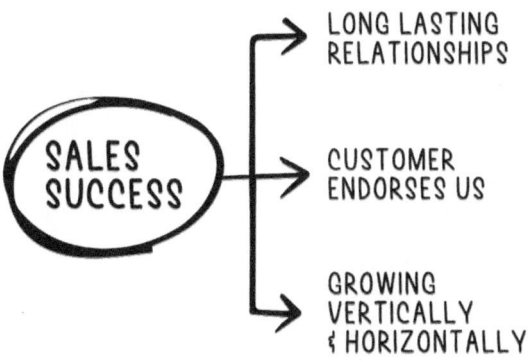

The beauty of challenges is that they make your success worthy. Just remember how happy you'd be when you succeed, knowing that you worked hard to make it happen.

> **"Challenges make you discover things about yourself that you never really knew"**
>
> **– Cicely Tyson**

Ask any successful person how he achieved success, how he overcame challenges in his journey. Now, ask the same person if given a chance to go back in time, would he/she like to avoid the greatest challenges they faced, the first time around? The majority of the people would give "No" for an answer to the second question. The reason being, it is through our biggest challenges that we sculpt ourselves into successful human beings. Challenges and obstacles are all a necessary part of any successful journey.

The Challenges in Sales

Will it be wrong if I say that the following three are the biggest challenges that a sales Person in any business or any industry has to face?

Challenge No. 1- Generation of leads

Challenge No. 2- Conversion of leads to business

Challenge No. 3- Getting repeat business

Some of you may say, fear of rejection, price objection, competition, lack of repeat business, etc. would be the challenges. Yes, each one of you is right, but all these are the barriers that lead to the three challenges that I have mentioned.

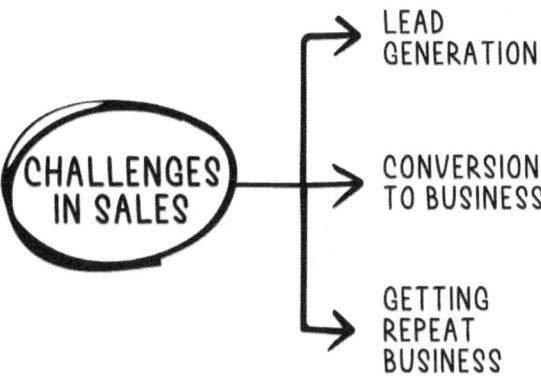

My 30 years of experience in the space of sales and marketing has made me meet thousands of salespersons, during these interactions and with a blend of my real-life experiences, I reckon the majorly faced challenges in the following three facets-

Generation of Leads

- Where to get the leads?
- Classification and identification of leads.
- Entry Barriers- Responses such as NOT INTERESTED or HAPPY WITH EXISTING VENDOR or WHY SHOULD I SHIFT TO YOUR BRAND?
- Fear of Rejection.

Conversion of Leads to Business

- The process of sharing what you can offer to the customer and what his needs are.
- Understanding those needs.
- Making productive presentations or calls
- What will make the difference in enhancing the quality of your presentation?
- Different buyers with different personalities and behaviors
- Objections, Several + Different
- Everything stops at price, doesn't it?
- Finally getting the order and making the sales

Getting Repeat Business

- You get the order, but will your customer buy again from you?
- Creating a relationship with our customer.
- Relationship management

Most of these challenges have been covered later in the workbook.

Another Perspective!

If you notice, that the challenges I mentioned above, are faced at different phases of a Customer's journey with you. At any given point in time, your customer could be at any one of the three stages mentioned below:

- **Acquisition** – the phase of mapping, prospecting, pitching, presentation, and converting the lead into customers
- **Retention** – the phase of servicing the customer, ensuring that he is delivered what was promised, at the time and at the cost it was promised. This is also the stage when the customer is engaged with consistent conversations regarding new solutions, range of products or services, value additions, promotions and participation.
- **Endorsement** – this is the stage of mature relationship with your customer and it is not the end of it. This is when the customer is loyal, trusts you and your solutions, has a level of dependency for his work and you enjoy a professional reputation in his eyes. This is the stage when he is going to refer to his network that gets you more business. This is true success in sales, your success.

'Be willing to allow the challenges to become your motivation'

Where there's success, there are bound to be challenges. That's the law of the universe.

Activity & Take Away

Prepare an excel sheet segregating your clients on the basis of the stages they are at, viz. Acquisition, Retention, or Endorsement. Following is an example for you to follow. You may add another column to mention the business per month from the customer or potential business per month from the prospect.

This will help you map on the exact status of where you are and the gap that you have between now and where you want to reach.

	Customer name	Phase	Status
1	Customer 1	Retention	Client since April 2019
2	Customer 2	Retention	Client since January 2018
3	Customer 3	Acquisition	Prospect. Sample under development - order from June 2020
4	Customer 4	Acquisition	Prospect. Order expected from June 2020
5	Customer 5	Acquisition	Presentation made, to follow up
6	Customer 6	Acquisition	Follow up going on
7	Customer 7	Acquisition	Waiting for appointment
8	Customer 8	Endorsement	Client since 2015. Has referred us to prospects - Customer 4 above
9	Customer 9	Retention	Client since May 2018
10	Customer 10	Retention	Client since December 2017

> **TIP: Another good exercise will be to list down the challenges that you face while selling.**
> **You can refer to this list as you move forward reading this workbook**

Revision

- Sales Success is achieved when your customers stay with you for long and they refer you to others
- To grow, ensure both horizontal expansion (getting new customers) and vertical (more sales to existing customers) business continues
- Each customer of yours is at one of these phases: Acquisition, Retention and Endorsement – and your growth plan depends upon where they are and where you want them to take

> **TIP: Consider you to be the owner of a business and act accordingly. This way you will be true to yourself and real.**

Notes

Chapter TWO

Always Be Prospecting

"Be an opener of doors"
– Ralph Waldo Emerson

Whatever level you may be working at, whether you are a sales executive, sales manager, business manager, business man or self-employed, ONE THING REMAINS COMMON – you need new business, new customers, every time. The question that springs up is- how do you capture new business and new customers? Do you remember Horizontal Expansion that we talked about in previous chapter?

Ask the following questions to yourself and give honest answers:

1. Do you get business from every new customer that you present to? Surely, the answer is "NO"
2. What is your productivity when you go out to sell? Can we express this in the form of percentage? 20% 30% 50% 70% - let us give it a fair chance and take 50% as the figure.

3. So if your productivity remains at 50%, how do you think you will achieve your numbers? Your target of achieving 100%?

That's where prospecting plays a key role.

Prospecting is a perpetual search for new customers by initiating contact with likely buyers through a series of mapping and marketing activities, including:

- Phone calls (cold calls)
- E-mails
- Social media
- Visits
- Social events
- Advertisements
- Websites and blogs
- Trade shows, exhibitions
- Please share, if you are using any other ways to initiate finding leads

The Golden Rule of Sales, without which no sales training or lecture or ultimately, selling is possible is called ALWAYS BE PROSPECTING which means one should always be looking for new prospects through referrals, through the available data, through events, through searching anywhere and everywhere. Because the fact remains that to have one new customer there have to be fifty prospects.

100 suspects

Give way to

50 prospects

That boils down to

25 presentations

Which may ultimately result in

1 sale

**Face the reality: Prospecting is hard
(but you've to make it enjoyable)**

ALWAYS BE PROSPECTING

Good intentions coupled with consistent action (in the right direction) result in business. Therefore, whether you are a sales rookie or an experienced salesperson, in the world of sales you definitely can't do without being organized, persistent, determined, and committed. Sunday or a Monday, every day is a prospecting day.

One important point - no one method of prospecting should be relied upon, a good salesperson opens several doors every single day.

In this chapter, we answer all the questions you've ever had regarding prospecting.

Prospecting is a process by which possibilities of working together are identified and explored. A prospect is identified and contacted to become a client. This is the stage of ACQUISITION where a prospect is identified, contacted, and then converted into a client.

Acquisition includes-

- Generating leads
- Cold calling
- Taking appointments
- Creating credibility
- Making presentations
- Generating interests
- Trial, orders and
- Follow-ups

Consequently, prospecting can precisely be called the gateway to acquisition.

But the process of prospecting doesn't start here. It begins much earlier than you think. It is not that one good day you will pick up a phone and start calling anyone, who is in business. You need to exactly know whom do you want to sell to, who is that prospect, who can give you business, not only once but for many, many years to come.

So you need to know where and how to generate your leads from and what type of leads do you require for your business. Please understand that lead generation forms the cornerstone of the entire process of acquisition and includes:

- Making of a sales plan

- Mapping the universe
- Segregating the leads

Let us take these components, one by one. Please go through and participate in this chapter with full intention and attention, as this will give you a solid base for your future sales success.

Make a Sales Plan

Making a Sales Plan is the basic groundwork that you can't do without. It will help you to gain clarity of the road that you take as you move forward in creating business. Let's begin to write 'My Sales Plan'; you write yours as I write mine. Don't forget, it's a workbook; you need to do the activities as we move along.

Answer the following questions on a spreadsheet or an excel worksheet:

1. Products and/or services that you (or want to) sell
2. Who is your target customer; whom all can you include in your list of prospects. You mention the categories or the industries that your prospects operate in.
3. The markets in which your products/services will be sold. Differently speaking, which are the geographical locations where your target prospects are situated
4. Which are channels that you will use to sell your products/services? You may have to choose among Dealer-Distributor Network, Direct selling, Multi-Level Marketing, or online.

5. Is there any seasonal impact on sales of your business? If yes, factor it in.

6. How much volume of your products or value of your services may be sold in which locations, to which prospects, when and through whom can be sold. And at what price? If you put all this information together, you will get your sales plan and it will look something like, what is illustrated below:

Table 1: Expected Sales over Locations:

- *We have shown only zones, you should make it by prospects and by cities, to have a detailed plan.*
- *Those cities will give you the following table as a resultant.*
- *If you intend to sell globally, choose those locations.*

	North India	East India	West India	South India
Product 1				
Product 2				
Product 3				
Product 4				
Product 5				
Total				

Table 2: Expected Sales over Months:

* *We have taken a financial year; you may choose the period that works for you.*
* *Ideally, you should make it for three years, as you may have to factor in, the repeat sale coming from existing customers in the 2nd and 3rd year.*
* *This table should reflect the seasonal impact, if any.*

	Apr	May	Jun	Jul	Aug	Sep	Oct	Nov	Dec	Jan	Feb	Mar
Product 1												
Product 2												
Product 3												
Product 4												
Product 5												
Total												

Table 3: Expected Sales, Zone wise over Months:

- *This will be an outcome of the Table 1 and Table 2*

	Apr	May	Jun	Jul	Aug	Sep	Oct	Nov	Dec	Jan	Feb	Mar
North												
East												
West												
South												
Total												

Was it difficult for you to visualize your sales numbers, without having even begun to sell?

Yes, it is not easy. But it becomes easier to plan if you use the technique of Benchmarking.

Now, what is that?

Benchmarking is a technique by which you may have a direct competitor-to-competitor comparison of a product, service, process, or method. For example, when I was working in Luxor-Parker pens and Parker pens were to be launched, we benchmarked the placement of Gillette Sensor Shaving Razor. We believed that Parker pens at a price of Rs.100 to 250 (year 1998) could be placed in shops that were selling Gillette sensor, other than the stationery shops selling premium writing instruments.

So when you make this plan, make sure that you benchmark it against the leader in the category or someone you look up to and wish to be like.

As you move along in this workbook, you will know how important it is to make the Sales Plan and that the effective plan will evolve by the time the workbook gets completed.

Map Your Universe

Once you have developed your Sales Plan based on your understanding and benchmarking your business vis-à-vis the leader, you have to dive deep further. Pick up every city or zone and make a list of companies/organizations/individuals who can be your possible customers. Remember, I said previously to get one business converted you may have to reach out to more than 50 prospects. Therefore it is pertinent for you to make a large list of potential customers.

You search these prospects through your network, the Internet or you may choose to take services of Database Companies.

This part of the workbook is about **3Cs - COLLECT, COLLATE and CONNECT.** This is where you mark your territory, your sales territory, and the battlefield where you are going to create successes that you will be proud of.

- COLLECT- To identify where the business is and where the potential customers are and then building the data of potential customers
- COLLATE- Segregate the data based on industry/application/size/location/accessibility/ possibility of any other parameter that fits your business
- CONNECT- once the list is ready, you will have to connect with each one on the data to explore their needs, requirements, and challenges and to fix appointments for presentations. After talking to these potential clients, you will come to know their level of business and their interest in working with you. That is why you need to connect, everyone on the list, whether by calling him or her or writing a mail. I have detailed on how to make an impressive first call or writing an introductory mail in the annexure. You may refer to it while connecting with the prospect for the first time.

Analyze & Segregate the Data

{Hot – Warm – Cold}

So now when you're devoting a fair amount of time regularly to your potential customer database and exploring them to be your probable clients, the resultant plate could look like a platter that's full of anything and everything on offer.

Looking at the platter, you can now know, who really can be your customers and who may not ever be your customer in near future. You need to study these findings about your data and then segregate them as Hot, Warm or Cold Prospects. It is quite obvious that we will work upon the Hot leads first as they would be the easiest (or fastest) to be available for meetings, or they will be more open to new ideas.

While, you may completely depend on your own understanding, but I would like you to go through the following four parameters on which you can analyze your prospects to mark them as hot, warm, or cold.

The BANT Methodology

Here enters the concept of BANT, where the letters B, A, N, T each represent a set of criteria namely Budget, Authority, Need, Time respectively.

The qualified "Leads" are segregated into the yardsticks of HOT, WARM and COLD. Let's first understand the criteria.

Budget

The prospect has prepared a budget and is ready for disposal at any time a project proposal is approved by the management. You may initiate this conversation by asking the following:

- *Do you have a budget?*
- *How much is your budget?*
- *Willing to expand, are you?*
- *Any budget range?*

Authority

If you're in contact with the person who has the authority to say 'yes' or 'no' to the proposal, then give that lead another plus point.

Being in touch with a decision-maker or a decision influencer makes things easy and also saves a lot of time.

Need

When the need of a prospect is identified, this sends a signal of a brewing lead. So, while conversing if you could open a relationship and identify your potential customer's need and address it, plus one point straight away.

Time Frame

The time gap between the times you spoke with the prospect and the projected period of purchase of the new product or service also sends out a signal to you. For example, you're an exhibition booth fabricator and your probable customer shows interest in your company based on communication with you but states that he has already finalized fabricators for the upcoming year, and will have the same requirement only after a year. Minus point 5, please!

That's no game that we're playing where now you'd sum up the score to look at the result. But the above-mentioned four traits help you classify your leads

A Hot Lead

A hot soup? Bring it on!!

A lead that meets 3 or 4 of the traits of BANT is a HOT Lead and should definitely be run after at full speed. You'll very well be able to make out through their conversation that they are the ones that are excited about your product or service and drop hints of collaboration.

A Warm Lead

A warm soup? Will do!

If the lead misses out on 1 or 2 of the 4 criteria, classify it as a warm lead. Take a note that here you most probably are able to identify a need; budget and time may be missed out on. They'd show interest in your product but would sound non-committal. However, warm leads can still be nurtured and worked upon.

A Cold Lead

A cold soup? Sorry, but NO!

If the lead misses out on 2 or 3 criteria, classify it as a cold lead. A cold lead won't be excited and won't even act excited. They'll require a lot of effort to be converted into a customer.

Since the time that you have to finish your meal is not perpetual, therefore an efficient professional makes a choice, one that's result-oriented, with most of the time being spent on the Hot Leads, comparatively less on Warm Leads and very little on Cold Leads.

Business success is not achieved overnight. It takes efforts, tools, skills, and strategies to achieve the desired results. Look at every lead as an edible opportunity to satiate your hunger. This gives way to a **SUCCESS DASHBOARD**, an important follow-up tool to ease your life.

Create Your Own Success Dashboard

Record your data – segregate them as HOT – WARM – COLD

Date	Prospect Company	Contact	Place	Phone	Email	Status
10/12	ABC & Company					HOT
10/12	XYZ & Company					WARM
10/12	True Company					HOT
11/12	Good Power House					COLD
11/12	Sincerely Yours					COLD

Take Away

Phew! It was a big chapter, with so much to plan. But this chapter is the foundation for building your sales success.

So do not forget to keep ticking the ones you have done

- ☑ Prospecting
- ☑ Preparing your Sales plan
- ☑ Benchmarking plays an important role to prepare a smart sales plan
- ☑ Segregation of your database into Hot, Warm & Cold leads based on BANT Methodology
- ☑ Create your Success Dash Board of Hot-Warm-Cold leads and approach them accordingly

Bonus!!

Once you've collected all the necessary data about the prospect (his company, key people of the company) and provided you are well versed with your own offerings (nothing less than a thorough knowledge would do); you're ready to make your first impression

So now you PICK UP THE PHONE!

Call up to take an appointment or for sellers, who are working in dealer network, reach to the shop, and make the first impression.

But, are you ready to make your first impression?

Prepare yourself for probable discouraging answers that you may have to face while you're on the call. Some of the discouraging replies may go like this -

- We are not interested
- Send me an email of your profile, I'll check
- We already have our supplier in place
- Call me later

These are nothing, but barriers to enter. What do you do then?

Make buyers interested from the beginning! The first impression is the last impression? Nah! **"The first impression is the lasting impression"**. Make your first impression, the LASTING impression for that will help you develop customer relationships and make sales.

---

5 tips for making a good first impression:

- **Your opening statement must grab the prospect's attention.**
- **Get to the point immediately.**
- **Your opening statement must be a beneficial statement.**
- **Always put yourself in the receiver's position as you develop your script. Customize it.**
- **Anticipate response from the receiver's perspective.**

Tip – Know your prospect before you call

Notes

_____

_____

_____

_____

_____

_____

_____

_____

_____

_____

_____

_____

_____

_____

_____

_____

_____

_____

_____

_____

_____

_____

_____

_____

_____

Chapter THREE

Effective Presentation

"You don't close a sale, you open a relationship"

– Patricia Fripp

Once you convince your prospect to meet you, you must gear up for an effective presentation. The objective is to understand about their business, their requirement, and their problem and then to offer them the right solution. Making a presentation to tell about your company, your products and services, your credibility and that how you would be the best solution provider for their problem.

But, I would like to give you a word of caution here. Your first meeting with the prospect is not about closing the sale; rather it is about opening a relationship. I have seen that salespersons spend all their time telling about themselves (and try to impress) the prospect with their achievements and solutions. But remember, Sales is about a best-fit solution.

Therefore, when you go to meet your prospect, please try and get the maximum information about them and then propose them the best-fit solution. For me, that is the meaning or the definition of Selling.

The questions that you need to ask the prospect:

- What they do?
- How they do it?
- When they do it?
- Where they do it?
- Why they do it?
- Who do they do it with?

The information thus collected, will give you insight into the gaps, the pain areas, and the challenges that your prospect has in his business.

Once you have taken the above information you will be sharing about your credentials, products, and offerings, and convince the prospect that how you (and your company) can help them and that it makes sense to do business with you.

To convince this your prospect, you better make sure that your presentation is very effective. And to do that, you must carefully understand what I have included in this chapter.

THIS INFORMATION WILL GIVE YOU INSIGHT INTO
PROSPECT'S NEEDS, GAPS & PAIN POINTS

Few quick pointers:

- When you're meeting your prospect for the first time, you must be ready with an effective presentation that strikes a chord with the client.
- Gather an idea of what you're going to say. Something that has worked in the previous meeting with some other prospect may/may not work with this prospect. Every prospect has unique concerns therefore your presentation must have specific content
- Don't overstress. Remember that they've invited you to come, meet and greet with them so they must think that you've something good to say.
- You'll have to don a hat of a person who believes in balancing acts, behave friendly and seem approachable. Open up conversations without coming across as an overly keen person.
- The outcome of presentation should be an agreement for "it makes sense to do business with us."

Remember, I gave you the rule of 'Always Be Prospecting' in the previous chapter. That was to ensure that your pipeline for growing sales is always filled. Similarly, here is another Golden Rule of Sales **'Always be Prepared'**.

So, what is it that you need to prepare for, to meet your prospect?

- Know your company and product offerings
- Know your prospect
- Define your goal of the presentation
- Prepare for potential objections

- Prepare your answers for those objections
- Prepare a Checklist of things that you need to ensure before the meeting

Let us discuss these points one by one.

Know Your Company and Product Offerings

If you're a salesman, your topmost responsibility should be to gather thorough knowledge about your company and then, your product or the service that you're selling. Note down all the queries that a prospect may have on a single piece of paper and then prepare how you're going to tackle that. Once you're ready, engross your colleagues and this is when the activity begins. Do a mock call before the real one

Assuming, your colleague is your prospective client. Approach him like you would approach your client. Go ahead with your presentation. Not only would you be able to gather feedback on your presentation but this would also serve as a practice ground and may give you more questions that you need to be prepared with.

Know Your Prospect

After your mock call practice, and learning about your offerings, the next is to learn about your prospect. You must prepare to learn about your prospect, to whom you intend to make a presentation.

With Google to our rescue, getting to know someone is just a click away. Try and find an insight about his credibility from other suppliers of products. During the presentation engage the prospect in a conversation and this is when you define your prospect's goal of having you over for the presentation.

He might be looking for a cheaper option, as you are the manufacturer or wants a better service. This is your turn! Once you know his goal, you've to smartly unite your goal to sound like his goal. Come up with a convincing answer to all his objections. Prepare for potential objections that your prospect may raise.

Define Your Goal of the Presentation

Do we really need to have a goal for the presentation? Yes, No or Maybe? But why do we need a goal?

As I said that the first goal of your first meeting is to know your prospect and his pain areas so that you can offer him the best-fit solutions. But is true when you are meeting them for the first time. But form subsequent meetings may have a different goal.

Let me take few examples.

- Your first meeting with the prospect has gone good, and you have understood the gaps and requirements. In your second meeting, you have to present the solution and share why should the prospect be buying from you? The goal of this presentation is to share the best-fit solution, using your knowledge
- You do that well and may be in the third meeting your goal is to close the deal.
- Or when you meet your existing customer to sell him a new product that your company has recently launched, your presentation will focus on the new offering

Once we learn to customize our presentations according to the goal, the chances of conversion improve. Of course, one has to learn to handle objectives and efficiently closing the calls and that is what will be covered in this workbook.

Prepare for Potential Objections and Preparing Answers for Those Objections

There is a separate chapter related to Objections and that offers tips to handle the objections. However, what we need to be prepared for are the possible questions that the prospect could ask. And you should know the answers as this will make you confident and professional.

Prepare a Checklist of Things That You Need to Ensure Before the Meeting

And you must ensure that all the boxes in the checklist are ticked.

Check-List

- Prospect Website checked
- Social Media pages and profiles of prospects checked
- Sales Kit ready

Sales Kit is the most important equipment for your meeting. Your sales kit must be up to date with all the necessary documents as listed below:

- ☑ Company Profile
- ☑ Brochures & Catalogs
- ☑ Technical details

- ☑ Cost sheets
- ☑ Samples
- ☑ Sales Presentation
- ☑ AV Film
- ☑ PPT
- ☑ Your Business Cards
- ☑ Notebook – to take notes

Tip: Do a time check. How much time do you have for the presentation?

Plan your presentation accordingly.

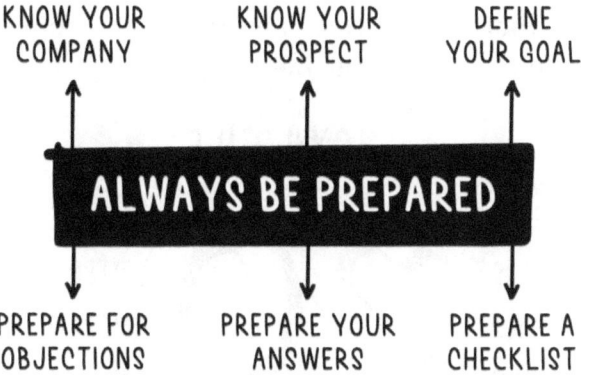

KNOW YOUR COMPANY

KNOW YOUR PROSPECT

DEFINE YOUR GOAL

ALWAYS BE PREPARED

PREPARE FOR OBJECTIONS

PREPARE YOUR ANSWERS

PREPARE A CHECKLIST

Plan – Prepare – Perform

Now that you are all geared up for the meeting, everything planned and your first meeting is all set. You are there at your prospect's office and waiting to be invited inside the room.

What are you doing at this moment? You could be doing a revision of questions that you have prepared for (like the last-minute look at the notes, before an exam!) or you could be looking around, observing the surroundings. Look around for any Awards or Certifications on the walls, or check the detailing and quality of interiors.

This is a part of a well-known concept called, 20x4 Rule for Sales Presentation. Go through this concept, make sure that you adhere to the rules and this shall prepare you to play a winning game at the meeting.

20X4 RULE

FIRST	**20**	INCHES
FIRST		STEPS
FIRST		SECONDS
FIRST		WORDS

First 20 Inches - The first (or top) 20 inches of your appearance include your hair and face that should always be well-groomed. You should smile; your mouth shouldn't smell bad and make sure to carry a deodorant for body odor that tends to kill the deals.

First 20 Steps - The first 20 steps should be practiced and worked upon. Your walk should exuberate confidence and happy vibes. In other words, your walk has to be impressive in order for you to walk through a deal. The jump in your walk shows the confidence that you have.

First 20 Seconds - The first 20 seconds govern how seriously your prospect would take you. 20 seconds is what you get before you land up in the chair in front of your prospect. As mentioned above, observe the walls, Awards, Certificates, paintings, etc. as these could be your opening point for your conversation.

First 20 Words - The first 20 words that you speak in front of the prospect will define the course that your presentation takes. Choose the opening words smartly and you will have your prospect talking. Speak clearly - speak effectively.

TIP: Attend to the basics – the 20x4Rule
From the moment you approach a customer, your behavior, attitude, and personal presentation will influence your customer's decision to buy.

Here is your moment to give your winning shot!

This section will give you tips for playing an efficient game with your prospect. Remember, what I mentioned in the earlier chapter, the first meeting is about knowing your customer and his needs. Through the process of presentation, use the following tips to enhance your performance.

TIP: Open Strong

Your opening statement must have a strong message that drives credibility and has a hook of making the client wants to know more.

- The opening statement can start with a congratulatory remark on their achievement or Award that you read on the website or on the wall. OR
- I had been waiting for this opportunity to meet up with such a senior and experienced person like you. Thank you so much for your time. OR
- I had been noticing your booth since the last three exhibitions and have always thought who had been getting such impressive work done!
- Make sure it should not be a fake statement – or you will get caught.

TIP: For making your presentation successful

Just a reminder – the success of your presentation depends upon:

- **Your Focus:** which should be more upon opening a relationship than closing a sale
- **Your Problem Solving Skills:** We want him to DECIDE to buy from us.
- **Your Willingness:** We don't have to sell – we help him to choose us.
- **Your Words:** Ask Open ended Questions

TIP: Ask open-ended questions

As stated before, the very concept of first impression, the first meeting is to open a relationship. You, as a salesperson, have to help him (the prospect) to choose you. Creating a conversation using open-ended questions is a great way to identify opportunities. You need to pave and lead the client in the direction "you" want them to take.

Open-ended questions are the questions that do not have a definite YES or NO as the answer. They start with Who, What, Where, When, Why, How, How much, Tell me more about, Describe for me. The aim of indulging in open-ended questions is to make the prospect feel like he's driving the conversation, it takes the conversation away from a typical yes or no and only detailed descriptions are spoken about.

Some open-ended questions, to which one can't reply to in the form of yes/no are-

- What type of product are you interested in?
- What are you looking for, in a quality provider?
- What's important to you in this decision-making process?
- How soon are you looking at implementing this?

- What is important to you?
- What risks do you perceive?
- What are your expectations from a new vendor?
- How can we help solve their problems?
- What do you think about our company?
- What do they like and dislike about their existing vendor?
- How satisfied are you from their existing vendor with respect to after-sales service?
- What is our next step?

At times we are not sure if the prospect will answer so many questions; we on our own think that this will sound like interrogation!!

If I had to do the same I will be very candid and say something like, "Thank you for your time Mr. Chopra and I would like to use this opportunity primarily for understanding your business so that I can offer the best solution from the world-class range of products that our company has to offer. It will be great if you answer some of my questions." And then I will ask my set of questions.

You can also do the same, go-ahead try it.

The key questions to be asked are:

- Tell me a little bit about your business?
- What is your company's point of difference in today's marketplace?
- Why do customers buy from your organization?
- Who else besides yourself might be involved in the decision-making process?
- What is the process of new vendor development?

TIP: Indulge in story-telling and building credibility

Don't start with the company profile in a 'matter-of-fact' fashion. Rather, start with a story or a strong startling fact. For example, Angad is into 'furniture business', so when he talks about his new business to his architect customers, he could or rather, should start with *"Our new business is an extension of Delhi NCR's largest furniture concept company"*

Or

"I have a concept which will bring art at affordable prices for your customers, while you make your share of profits and credibility"

Starting with stories doesn't mean that the facts are not being told. Whatever we open with has to be substantiated with facts, figures, data, certifications, brochures, images, and other factual details that add to the credibility.

TIP: Add examples and success stories

Talk about the previous time a consumer availed your services and how he immensely benefited. Talk about his benefit, because that's all he's interested in.

TIP: Do not overwhelm the prospect

No misleading stories, no false promises would do. Your total focus has to be HIM, the prospect. Focus on his products and services, not yours.

TIP: Listen 80%, Speak 20%

Reminder: Your main aim during the first meeting is to 'open a relationship'. Therefore, you've to let the prospect walk the talk. Keep the first meeting conversational.

TIP: Take Notes

Jot down on a piece of paper what the prospect has to say. It's an action that shows that you're interested and can't afford to miss out on any single detail. These notes will help you to prepare the minutes of the meeting to share with the prospect.

TIP: Be FABulous: Features. Advantages. Benefits.

Because when you talk FAB, you get FAB results. It is as simple as that.

Under the FABulous technique, the focus remains more on the Benefits in comparison to the features (and advantages). FAB emerges out as the simplest yet the most effective technique of conversation. The best part about the same is that this technique works out in any sales environment, be it retail, B2B or B2C. Let's understand the FABulous technique with the help of an example.

Your company makes non-bloating, mineral water, and your role is to sell them to 4-5 Star hotels. The things that you must know (about your company and the product):

- The brand name is "M-QUA"
- M- stands for Minerals that it has and QUA – is for water (AQUA)
- The product has energy boosting minerals

- The water is non-bloating which means that one doesn't feel 'full & heavy' after drinking M-QUA
- It is available in 500ml bottles
- The bottle design is such that it can be crushed manually after us and folds to one-fifth size
- It is priced at 150% of the regular packaged water (without minerals and non-bloating pricing)

Now you have to sell M-QUA to the F&B Manager of a 5 Star Hotel

While making your presentation, you may focus on the benefits of M-QUA being placed at their hotel. Let me show you how?

M-QUA is non-bloating – that's a feature and it improves appetite is the advantage and that – the guests will not feel full during meals and that they will eat better (more) which would mean more billing. Now this surely will interest the Hotel, more billing.

M-QUA has minerals - that's a feature and it gives energy is the advantage and that – your guests remain happy and enthusiastic while staying with you is the benefit that the Hotel could be interested in.

Placing the bottles in Gym area will also increase billing because of the above-mentioned features. Why would your prospect not get excited?

The difference in pricing can be subdued because of these benefits that M-QUA has to offer.

This was a very simple example to help you understand the concept of focusing on the emotional benefits instead of features and advantages.

The idea is simple. There is no competitive advantage in defining features. Advantages are functions of features, doesn't excite the prospects any more.

Amazing part is that the benefits should also be the same if the features are the same and the advantages will also be the same and why should the benefits not be the same.

This is because the needs of the customer would be different. For needs of customer in 5star hotel, which caters to the elite and foreign tourist will be different from a premium standalone specialty restaurant and to an in-flight service menu.

FEATURES   ADVANTAGES   BENEFITS

BENEFITS ENGAGE.
THEY MAKE THE PROSPECTS INTERESTED

Activity

On a sheet of paper, jot down the features, advantages and benefits respectively of the product or service that you sell.

Take Away

It was a long chapter with so many components. I hope you take away important elements from this chapter and make your presentation worthwhile.

- Always be prepared – prepare the checklist and adhere to it
- **Good luck is the result of good planning!**
    - Planning gives you CONFIDENCE
    - Planning enables you to FORSEE OBJECTIONS
    - Planning makes you hold an ADVANTAGE OVER THE PROSPECT
    - Planning enables you to POSITIVELY SUGGEST ORDER QUANTITY/PRODUCT/PROCESS
    - Planning makes you PROFESSIONAL in the eyes of the prospect

- Define the Goal of your presentation
- Remember – we want the prospect to DECIDE to buy from us, and as a salesperson, we help him do that
- Remember the 20 x 4 Concept
- Open strong – the first impression makes a lasting impression
- Ask open-ended questions while understanding the client
- Presentation is about creating conversations – including story telling, success stories, examples to build credibility
- Listen 80% - Talk 20%
- Take Notes during presentation

- Be FABulous –Focus on Benefits and not features or advantages
- Prepare – practice - present

MIND IT: THE WILL TO WIN IS WORTHLESS IF YOU DO NOT HAVE THE WILL TO PLAN, PREPARE OR PRACTICE

Notes

Chapter FOUR

The Fourth Vowel – The Big 'O'

In our previous chapter, we took an example of M-QUA mineral water, which was to be presented to the F&B Manager of a Hotel. I am sure, if presented in reality, the Hotel Manager would have asked few questions, like why should it be more expensive than what he is already buying, or logistics or would have asked for samples. These questions are generally mistaken (by the Salesperson) as Objections.

This chapter pertains to the fourth vowel, the letter O. The big O. But, don't worry, read this chapter to convert the big O of sales, i.e., the 'Objections' into a bigger O, i.e. the 'Opportunities'

What are Objections?

Objections are nothing but Opportunities. Objections are a tinge of hint that points out that your prospect has heard you. He may/may not have heard all of what you've said but there's something that has been caught up in his brain. So, congratulate yourself (Of course, inside your head).

Just imagine, you make a presentation to the prospect and he has nothing to say or ask. What could this mean? In all probability, he hasn't heard you at all or he has chosen to ignore it. Is this an indication that the possibility to convert the prospect into a customer is over?

So you should feel happy if your prospect asks some questions. Whether on benefits, prices, or logistics, it's good news for you. This is how you surge ahead.

Objections – True or False?

Once you get an objection – try and see if the objections are true or false, because you'd know.

Let's take the same example of M-QUA.

If you want to replace Bisleri with M-Qua, the prospects telling you that it will be too expensive for their customers – that is quite a valid objection. But, the same objection, if raised by a 5-star hotel – it may not be true as he is anyway selling at a premium. If the objection is about the buying price of M-Qua, which is higher than their existing brand, the objection sounds valid and you need to address that.

But I repeat that to have an objection by the prospect is good news. However, there is a reverse perspective to look at the objections.

You must have come across on many occasions that the prospects and the customers tend to be rude or ask 'funny' questions (that is what we think) or unrelated questions, or get irritated or snub you? These are negative objections and you land up thinking 'Why?' Where I have gone wrong?

How many of you have faced this ever in your experience? Remember that time and now go through the next part of this chapter, it will be more relatable.

Before we try and understand the ways of handling objections, it will be important for us to understand the root-cause that lead to negative objections.

What causes Objections?

An objection could be a result of a lot many factors. From the prospect's reluctance to your lack of preparedness, the objection in the mind of a prospect could arise due to:-

- Poor presentation
- Lack of preparedness
- Lack of product knowledge
- Lack of company knowledge/policies
- Personal reasons (Speech/Appearance/Manner/ Attitude)
- Objections created to get rid of you

How to handle Objections?

As mentioned earlier, objections are nothing but Opportunities, even if they are negative objections. Therefore, the best way to handle objections is to LISTEN and listen patiently. So when your prospect starts stating his objections, there are certain aspects you've to be careful about. Here are the key points you need to be aware of-

- Do not interrupt
- Remain calm and not defensive
- Notice reactions
- Take notes
- Do not jump to conclusions
- Hold your temper (this one's is utmost importance)

Once you have lent ears to the entire objection or a list of objections, the handling part starts.

Take a pause of three seconds before you start responding, and then start answering. Let's understand this with the help of an example.

You are a Business Development Executive in an exhibition design & fabrication Company.

Your prospect is a medium-size Packaging Machinery Manufacturer. They are participating in a Packaging Industry Exhibition. They need to showcase 2 machines at their booth.

Objection: I understand that your work is good, but you have never earlier worked in our industry where we have to install machines in the booth and there is a lot of wiring done. We need at least 10 hours to set up and your lack of experience may become a barrier.

Now how do you address this objection?

I would answer it like this: Yes you are right that we have never worked in your industry, packaging machinery is new to us. But if you notice that we have worked in a similar situation (in Paper Exhibition) wherein the required time was only a day to set up a machine and we did it efficiently. And then I would show them the image of the past experience. And for us in our experience of 12 years, we have worked for 24 different industries, so every time we have learned about the category and performed accordingly.

That's an ideal scenario that brings us to two objection handling techniques that rarely fail. I will take them one by one.

Yes, But ... Technique

The trick here is to 'Agree with the Objection'. Say YES! And then add 'But'

- Yes, you are correct – But...
- Yes, I agree with you – but...
- Yes, that is possible – but...
- It is a very good idea – but...

You noticed in the example above, I started with 'Yes, you are right'. The moment you agree to the objection, the prospect gets a little comfortable and opens up to listen further.

Just think, if the answer was, "No sir, you did not see my presentation properly. We have done a similar project in Paper Exhibition where the time was less. But we did it well sir. We have an excellent team sir; we have not gone wrong ever."

What is wrong with this? Read once again. You just blamed the prospect of not having seen the presentation properly!! Get ready for a fight now; he is going to pull your arrogance down by argument.

TIP - Never start your answer with a 'No'

To say this differently – Never say 'No' to start your answer. Avoid statements like, "No, you're wrong" OR "You don't understand". That's the worst that you can say to your prospect.

Probing/Digging Technique

As the name suggests, this technique is about finding more, diving deep into understanding of the objection. Go ahead, dig deeper, and inculcate phrases in your conversation that ask more from the prospect, make sure to raise valid points.

Use phrases like:

- Apart from that...
- Let's assume that...
- Suppose that...

Could this technique be used in our example of Exhibition? Let's try the possible answers.

- *Apart from your questions* regarding our lack of experience in your category, is there any other concern that you have. Please be assured that our award-winning fabrication team will do a great job of your booth.
- *Let's assume* that this concern of yours is taken care of is there anything else that bothers you?
- *Suppose that* we take complete responsibility for delivering what we promise and we shall take only 50% advance (instead of normal 75%) for the project, will that help?

Don'ts of Objection Handling

So, when the prospect has raised an objection about your product or may be regarding your presentation of the product, you can't go about stating that the prospect's objections are baseless or false. Here's a list of what's not to be done:

- Do not contradict/flatly deny an objection
  - *No sir, that is not true, we are better priced than you think*

- Do not use words that antagonize
  - *No sir, you didn't understand...*

- Do not make false promises
  - *Sir, I will not take any advance for this project (Just for your knowledge, in exhibitions, people don't work without advance)*

- Do not argue- this one's the most important
  - *No sir, what you are saying is absolutely wrong... I can prove it*

I hope you have understood the message that I want to give. Objections take the conversations forward don't break the flow by not handling that properly.

Take away

◆ Welcome objections your way because they're nothing but opportunities.
◆ **Do Not Argue.**

NO SALESMAN EVER WINS AN ARGUMENT
EVEN IF HE WINS, HE LOOSES THE PROSPECT

Activity

Managing the first Objection

Suppose you're trying to fix the first meeting with the prospect, on a phone call. What would your answer be if you were faced with the following objections?

1. We are not interested
2. We already have our supplier in place
3. Send me an email with your profile
4. I'm too busy to think about it
5. I've never heard of your company
6. Call me back later in the year
7. We don't have any budget left this year

I will be happy to receive the responses!

Notes

Chapter FIVE

Seal the Deal

Just imagine, you have made the presentation, he (the prospect) has nodded in approval, and then it is all-quiet! The customer didn't utter a word, and you keep waiting for him to say something. To avoid the same awkwardness, he opens his mouth and you think, here comes the order. He opens his mouth to say – give me some time to think over. I shall call you back.

Here goes your brilliant presentation and the perfect objection handling out of the room. What follows is that you suddenly see yourself asking him to negotiate the price because you think that is the only reason that has not worked in your favor and your desperation starts showing up.

How many times have you succeeded to seal the deal immediately after making the presentation? Not always. Why not?

- Maybe because you did not handle objections properly
- Or maybe the client was actually not the decision-maker

- Or maybe your presentation was not too great
- Or maybe someone's prices were more competitive
- Or maybe.... there can be so many reasons...

But how many of a time has this happened that all the 'MAYBEs' didn't exist, you had the best price, best offering, had handled all the objections, the presentation was nothing less than perfect and the customer needed what we had to sell and he was the decision-maker – still we did not close the deal. Then, why?

That's when another may be arises. Maybe, you did not take charge of closing the call that you had opened. We think our job ends with the presentation and the customer's favorable reply is in the offing.

Take a note of the fact that we often fail because **we do not close the call at all**.

REMEMBER – the onus of closing the call is on us, the seller and not the buyer.

Maybe you close, by taking the responsibility of closing the call. But you did not close it effectively. What does this mean?

Let's again understand with the example, which we had stated above. Just imagine, you have made the presentation, he (the prospect) has nodded in approval, and then it is all-quiet. The customer didn't utter a word, and you keep waiting for him to say something, you become a little restless. You ask him, "what do you say?" and he opens his mouth. Here, comes the order, you think.

But!

He says, "Give me some time to mull over. I shall call you back."

So nothing has changed. You know why? Because we had asked him (the prospect) an open-ended question the answer to which could've been anything he had wanted.

Dear friends, these are the rules of the game. You ask open-ended questions when you open the call. But when you have to close the deal, you ask closed questions so that you get definitive answers.

TIP- Ask close-ended questions to close the call

So something was missing. And that was knowledge of techniques and tips for closing the call, which we will study in this chapter.

This is what we call the desired outcome of the presentation made to the prospect. To get sales, this is the winning post time. This is the logical end of a well-planned and well-executed presentation.

This is the difference between Success and Failure.

I have a question!

At the first meeting with a prospect, what would the word 'closing' mean?

CASE 1: Meeting the prospect with the objective of understanding them and their need. The first meeting, where the objective is to open a relationship, must end on a sweet note. What would 'Closing' mean here?

"I have understood your requirements, your problem areas, your concerns, and your expectations from us. In my understanding, you are satisfied with your present vendor, but I need to come back to you with the value additions. And I see this as a possibility because we are the leading players in our field."

Can we keep our next meeting on Wednesday, 13th December at around 3 pm? And if that is not possible, let's keep it for the morning, same day?

Great, I am putting it on my calendar. Thank you so much.

Another question!

What would the word 'closing' mean at the final meeting with the prospect?

In this case, possibly, you have had multiple meetings with the prospect; maybe you have shared some samples, given your best quotes, and today it seems that this one will be the one, when you will get the order. How do you think the closing shall be done?

But before I tell you about the closing techniques, here enters another golden rule into the picture. **The third and the most crucial 'Always' of selling is called 'ALWAYS BE CLOSING'.** Look for buying signals that your prospect has been dropping sporadically or maybe, incessantly.

When should one close?

There's no appropriate time for clinching a deal. As soon as you get a buying signal, don't let it go. Seize the occasion and advance in the direction of the deal.

What is a buying signal?

Buying signals are the cues that indicate the prospect's intentions or readiness to buy. Buying signals tend to make the sales process more logical and high yielding.

TIP- Don't take too long to close.

Some examples of what should definitely be considered as buying signals are:

- How long will it take you take to deliver?
- Is it possible to make this in olive green and black combination?
- Do you have a fabrication unit in Mumbai?
- What is your credit policy?
- Can I see a sample/demo?
- Can we have a group meeting with the rest of my team?

So keep your eyes and ears open to pay heed to the Buying Signal.

BUYING SIGNALS ARE QUESTIONS
THAT THE PROSPECT ASKS

The Tricks of the Trade - Closing Techniques

And just like objection techniques, there exist closing techniques that facilitate one to close a call efficiently. You choose and use one according to the situation.

There are many ways of closing a sale. One must take care of the fact that as a salesperson, it is our job to close and not that of the customer. Following 7 techniques must be on every salesman's scheme of things -

1. **Direct Close/Physical Action Close**
2. **Alternate Close**
3. **Trial Order**
4. **Concession Close**
5. **Verbal Proof Close**
6. **Pros & Cons Close**
7. **Door Knob Close**

Direct Close

A direct close is a straightforward request to the buyer to commit to a purchase.

This method should be used only when you're sure that the prospect would buy from you. This is used when you have built a good rapport with the prospect and can afford to be direct.

Example - **"Can I expect a PO coming from your end? I shall send the formal quotation for 100 cases today itself"**

CAUTION: Don't sound pushy assuming your rapport with the client to be good.

Physical Action Close

It is a different format of the 'Direct Close' technique that works really well in the dealer-distributor network while working with 'ready stock'. When you get an indication to buy & you are confident of the quantities given, you ask for the stocks, deliver, display and make the bill.

Alternate Close

This is one technique where you are not going to be too direct with the prospect. You give him a choice to make.

For example, you could be asking him, **"Can I raise a PI for 50 cases or 100 cases?"**

By giving him a choice, you are respecting his decision making power and surely forwarding him to close the deal.

Another point – in the choices that you have given, what do you think he will opt for? Most probably, he will choose for 50 cases. If we had been in his place, we would also have chosen the lower figure. That is human nature; we tend to opt for smaller figures when we have to place an order the first time. So offer the choices smartly.

Trial Order Close

Post your presentation and objection handling, when your prospect remarks that he's not sure of the quality, service or that he's satisfied with the services of his existing vendor, the 'Trial Order Close Technique' works well.

You can make a powerful comeback through your words by saying, **'as a trial order, can I book only 5 cases? You can try them in one week's production, your workers**

can also try it out and then we can take this further.
I am available for all the support to workers, in case they
have any trouble applying our products.'

This Trial Order Close; works really well while
launching a new product/pack to an existing customer
or while opening a new outlet, specifically in the dealer-
distributor category.

Concession Close

It so happens at times that the price of a particular product
acts as a deal barrier. The prospect desires some concession
before he can finally give a green signal to the sale.

For example, a small price reduction or a slightly
extended credit period for an immediate order could strike
a chord with the prospect. Here, you (the seller) show
that you are personally providing special service for that
particular prospect. But what you've actually done is that
you've encouraged the prospect to make a positive decision
by offering a concession (within the company policy)

**Concessions should be kept till the very end and
used only if necessary. This is because if a concession is
used too soon, or it is seen to be available to everyone,
its impact is lost.**

Verbal Proof Close

First of all, you've to realize that the word of mouth is really
a powerful tool and if you're not using the tool in your
business then you're definitely missing out on a huge chunk
of the audience. When you use the 'Verbal Proof Close', you
refer to an existing client (not competition) or a particular

application and highlight the benefits derived out of it and how they can benefit from the same. You support this claim in the form of a document or letter or any reference. To give creditability to our claim we may suggest the prospect to cross- check the claim.

For example, an exhibition booth fabricator could use documentary proof works to pitch in the sales, **"we had fabricated four booths in the same exhibition and one of them was awarded as the best booth in the category. Here is their testimonial."**

Pros & Cons Close

This is where you, as the salesman has to switch on to the entrepreneurial mode and think like a businessman. Pros & Cons Close is one of the most powerful of all closing techniques for a very simple reason. This method closely parallels the way you and I think and make decisions in every area of our lives. We weigh the pros and cons. We look at the reasons in favor of a decision and compare them with the reasons against making the decision.

Benjamin Franklin, America's first self-made millionaire, made this technique famous. He developed the habit of making his decisions by taking a piece of paper and drawing a line down the center. He would write all the reasons in favor of making the decision on one side of the paper, and all the reasons opposed to the decision on the other side. He would then study the lists, and make his decision.

This is how it works. Take a piece of paper and draw a line down the center. Now, let's write down all

the reasons in favor of making this purchase decision on the left-hand side."

Whenever you are selling anything complex or high capital investment product, this is an excellent method to use.

Just Suppose Close

'Just suppose' technique is your ultimate rescue when the prospect's key objection is the price. So when the prospect says that he can't afford what you are selling. You reply and say, **"Mr. Prospect, just suppose that price is not an obstacle and that we can deal with your price concerns to your complete satisfaction, should we consider this as deal. Or is there any other concern that we still have?"**

This technique may not give an on-the-spot closure but surely will open channels for more discussion towards closing the deal.

When you hear your prospect saying, "Wow, that's a lot of money," what he really means is: "You haven't given me enough reasons to justify that price". Remember that a price objection is really a price question. A price question is when he says, "That's too expensive." What he is asking is, "from what you've told me so far, I don't see how you can charge so much for your product or service. Can you give me some more information?"

> **TIP- Remember that it is not the price but the reasons for the price that are most important.**

You say, **"Mr. Prospect, it may sound like a lot of money, but let me tell you why it costs what it does, and**

why it is worth every penny." You proceed and explain the value of your product that more than justifies the amount you charge for it.

Be proud of your prices. When the prospect says things like, "It costs too much." Or, "You charge more than your competition." You say, "Mr. Prospect, you're right. As a matter of fact, it costs Rs.7800 more than our closest competition."

"And yet we sell thousands of these every year to very intelligent people like your good self. Would you like to know why?" You then go on to explain why people buy from you, and continue to buy, even at higher prices.

You have to get the price out of the way at the beginning. Other than that, it just sits there like a big orangutan in the middle of the path between you and the sales.

Door Knob Close - For a dash of a little drama!

The Door Knob Close is the technique that you use when you have almost lost the sale. You've made your presentation. You've given it your best shot. The prospect has resisted. The prospect still has that one major issue, that one major objection. They're not telling you, because they know if they tell you, you're going to answer it and make the sale.

You have said everything you can think of. "Is it the money that you're concerned about? How far apart are we? What do we have to do to make a deal today?" The prospect keeps saying, "No. I'm not sure. I want to think it over." But he won't tell you what it is that's stopping him from closing. You know that he can afford it, and that he likes it, and want it, and so on. Finally, you say, "Mr. Bhatia, thank you very much for your time. I know, today is not my day, I know how busy you are, and I appreciate your talking to me. I'll be on my way now. Will call up again to fix the time for next meeting."

You close your bag, get to your feet and go to the door. As you get to the door, you put your hand on the 'doorknob'. At this moment, the prospect gets a little relaxed as you are now going out of his room. His sales resistance drops. **But then, here comes the drama... You turn around and say, "Oh, by the way, just before I go, I was wondering about something.** I know that you're not going to buy anything today, but I wonder if you could help me with my sales presentation. Could you tell me, if there was a failure on my part to present my case, what was the real reason that you didn't buy today?"

Why would you do that? Just because at this point the prospect has become a little relaxed, you can catch him without any wall of resistance.

Often the prospect will say, "Well, I'll tell you. The real reason was this (he will give his reason)." At that point, you take your hand off the doorknob and you go back in. You set down your bag. You say, "Mr. Bhatia, I am so glad you told me that. That's my fault. Obviously, I didn't explain that part of our offering to you. May I go over that point just one more time?"

Now you have the key reason for not buying. If you can answer it effectively, you can close 50% and more of these lost sales.

The "funda" behind this sales technique is to catch the prospect in a brief moment during which he's in 'at ease' state. Therefore, not only this method contributes to your sale but also tells you why you were turned down in the first place.

So now you know how to convert your lost deal into a signed contract.

I hope you have understood these techniques and will keep them in mind while making your sales presentation. Remember that you have to choose the right technique based on the situation that you have during your presentation.

There is a big chance; and I mean a very big chance for you to close the sale, if you apply any of these closing techniques. You will have to take note of buyers' key reasons for buying or not buying and act upon them accurately. You may also club two or more of these techniques during your sales call and get results.

Always have a next step defined

The close is not your last sale to the client; this will help the completion of process.

Finalize the next step then and there. Fix the next meeting the same day; get it recorded on the prospect's smartphone so that it doesn't slip his mind. Tell him that you will call a day in advance and make sure that you send minutes.

These are a few of the most important tips in B2B business dealings.

Make sure that it is delivered, that is promised and within the lead-time. Integrity is integral for Sales Success. It is understandable that it may not always be possible to deliver as promised, but make sure that the customer is completely informed about the situation. This will build his trust in you.

Remember, you don't want to be the last dealing with your customer. Does ensuring the timely delivery guarantee you repeat business?

This is the question that I answer in the next chapter.

Take Away TIPS

- The onus of closing the call is on us, the seller, and not the buyer
- Always Be Closing – lookout for the buying signals from the prospect
- Ask closed-ended questions, while closing
- There are many techniques of closing – choose the one that suits the situation
- You can club the techniques if the situation demands
- After the closing make sure that you have a next step pre-decided.

Notes

Chapter SIX

Retention: The Key to Growth

Let me now take you back to Chapter One that talked about the challenges in sales. It included lead generation, conversion of lead to sales, and the third getting the repeat business. The first two challenges were addressed in previous chapters; I am going to talk about the last one in this one.

Getting Repeat Business

Another challenge that one encounters during sales pertains to repeat business. The first sale becomes a repeat customer only when he buys month after month or better said, repeatedly.

Of course your production department will do their best to offer them their best services – but will that ensure business? May be or maybe not, because out there is competition! Just like you, there are many good salesmen from competition, who are doing their job equally well – rather they are working on overtime to snatch away your buyer. So the question arises: how do you retain your customer?

What do you think is the differentiator? Here's your answer: Form a Relationship. Now, read the last three words again.

Form a Relationship

Be a collaborator. Be a solution provider and not just a vendor. As a collaborator, you have been able to sell the best-fit solution to the customer. You need to do that more often. Stay connected with the customer through the process of any or all of the developments that take place at the customer's end. Take ownership of your relationship with them.

Ask for feedback

Feedback - is said to be the breakfast of champions. Feedback provides you an opportunity to improve which is any day greater than more business. Recording a feedback post the final sale is important. Get back to your customer, ask if all is good, and then pick up the learning, if there exist any. You must act upon the negative feedback; include your seniors, your management, and get things sorted. Don't forget the idiom, the cost of finding a new customer is 10times more than an existing customer.

Stay Connected

Just one sale was not your ultimate purpose. Your ultimate purpose is to convert that one sale into repeated sales. Remember, vertical growth we talked about in Chapter one, that is a sure sign of sales success. Therefore, after the first sale, you must be visible, stay connected, and in communication.

So how do you stay connected throughout with the customer?

- E-mailers/Direct Mailers
- Company Newsletters
- Invitations to company events, conferences and exhibitions
- Engage them in your Company's Social & CSR initiatives
- Festivals and special occasions
- Special Offers
- The client's special occasions
- LinkedIn

TIP: Connect with your clients for at least 6 times a year.

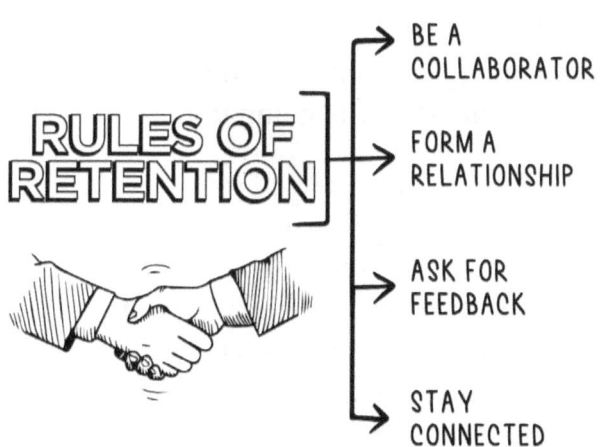

RULES OF RETENTION

→ BE A COLLABORATOR

→ FORM A RELATIONSHIP

→ ASK FOR FEEDBACK

→ STAY CONNECTED

Track Your Customers' Performance

Your success dashboard helps you to maintain a thoroughly analyzed data, track your client's business progress and create a report analysis weekly or monthly. You can now easily see if your key customers are continuously buying and that you are always prospecting.

In case you see a deviation, connect with your customer and find out the reason. Address the concern and bring your business back.

Ask for reference and endorsement

As you progress in your business of sales, a time will come that some of your key customers will be your largest contributing customers. You will have a matured business relationship developed with them, which will be built on mutual trust and reliability. This is the stage where they will be open to endorse you and your company to others.

Once you have reached that stage with the customer that is when you will be allowed to flaunt your greed. So, go ahead, be greedy, and ask for your client's reference and endorsement. Not only would that let you know your strong points but also it is going to take your business to the next level.

Take away

It is important to retain a customer by staying connected with them throughout and maturing to a point of making them your key customer. But it is not a one-time task; it is perpetual. Here are some of the important takeaway tips to make that happen:

- Form a relationship with your customer
- Stay connected and be a collaborator
- Be the Solution Provider and not a seller

- Connect at least six times in a year
- Track your customer's business with you
- Connect with them immediately in case you see a deviation in performance
- Be greedy and ask for references and endorsements

Bonus!

Technology at your command to help you succeed!

I have seen the world changing in the last 30years of my working experience. I started when there were no computers, everything was manual and we used to create lead generation data from printed yellow pages, industrial association directories, newspaper classifieds, and all primitive routes to source data.

And to retain the customer for long we would depend on direct mailers, newsletters, greeting cards, phone calls and personal meetings.

In modern times, information & digital technology has altered the way we do sales, generate leads, and retain customers. There are many CRM (Customer Relationship Management) software available in the market which enable the companies to manage leads, track the follow-ups, customer performance and engage them over the business years.

And of course, there is social media, especially LinkedIn, which is a great place to connect with your leads and engage with your customers. If treaded carefully, it can create a wonderful professional network.

With digital calling, webinars, and video meetings becoming a part of the new normal, it would be a lot easier to connect with your customer.

A word of caution though, the best results can be achieved if we break the clutter of the digital world and stay focused on becoming the collaborator with the customer.

This will never fail you.

Notes

_____

_____

_____

_____

_____

_____

_____

_____

_____

_____

_____

_____

_____

_____

_____

_____

_____

_____

_____

_____

_____

_____

_____

_____

_____

_____

_____

The Final Words

**"Knowledge becomes wisdom only after it
has been put to practical use"**

I had a great time writing this workbook for you. I hope you also had a good time working through it. My intention in writing this workbook was to remind you that what you miss when selling becomes a regular, mundane job to do. The idea was to bring some excitement back into the selling process. The tips and scenarios shared in the workbook were simple triggers for you to get excited, and I hope the goal was achieved.

To Ensure Success,

Practice- Practice- Practice

Make sure that you use the tips that you have been given on everyday basis. It is the practice and your intention to practice that's the most important reason to ensure your success.

But I also know that practice to practice is the most difficult aspect of this commitment. But if you want to put this learning to use, you will have to be more demanding to yourself.

Make a Choice. Soar high. All the best.

I shall wait for your feedback about the Workbook.

Rajeev Narang

Summary of Workbook for Your Ready Reference

GET UP ARiSE
Boost Your Sales Success

Selling is about asking (or knowing) from the prospect WHAT they do, HOW they do, WHAT they do, WHEN they do, WHERE they do it, WHY they do and do they do it with – and then helping them to do it better. Done in a way that the prospect believes that it makes sense to do business with you.

Tips to remember!

1. Sales Success happens when you grow
   a. Horizontally (adding more customers)
   b. Vertically (doing more business with existing customers)
2. A successful salesperson has
   a. Long-lasting relationship with his customers
   b. Customers endorsing and referring to new prospects
   c. Growing horizontally and vertically
3. Challenges in sales
   a. Lead generation

b. Conversion of prospects to customers

c. Retaining the customers

4. Always be prospecting

a. Keep your pipeline full

5. Client Acquisition includes the following, make sure you do that:

a. Make a sales plan

b. Mapping the universe

c. Segregate leads as HOT-WARM-COLD

6. Your first impression has to be a 'lasting' impression

7. Know your prospects before call

8. Always be prepared

9. Make sure you have a checklist before you go for a meeting AND actually check it

10. The 'Will to Win' is worthless if you do not have the 'will to plan or prepare'

11. Attend to the basics: the 20x4 Rule

a. Top 20 inches

b. First 20 steps

c. First 20 seconds

d. First 20 words

12. Following make your presentation successful:

a. Your focus on objective

b. Your problem-solving skills

c. Your willingness

d. Your words

13. Ask open-ended questions to open a new call

14. Open Strong – Create a WOW!

15. Add examples & success stories in your presentation to build credibility

16. Don't give misleading stories and don't make false promises

17. Listen 80% Speak 20%

18. Take Notes at the meeting and use them for minutes of the meeting for the client

19. Be FABulous

    a. Talk about benefits during your presentation. Benefits connect emotionally, more than features and advantages

20. Objections are nothing but opportunities

21. What causes objections?

    a. Poor presentation

    b. Lack of preparedness

    c. Lack of product/company knowledge

    d. Personal reasons – speech/appearance/attitude

22. How to handle objections?

    a. Do not interrupt

    b. Remain Calm and don't be defensive

    c. Notice reactions

    d. Do not jump to conclusions

    e. Do not start your answer with a NO

    f. Do not flatly deny the objection

    g. Do not argue - No salesman ever wins an argument, even if wins, he loses the customer

23. The ONUS of closing the call is on the salesman and not the customer

24. Ask close-ended questions to close the call

25. ALWAYS BE CLOSING – look for buying signals

26. Chose the 'closing technique' as per the situation

    a. Direct or Physical Action close

    b. Alternate close

    c. Trial Order close or Concession close

    d. Verbal Proof close

    e. Pros & Cons close

    f. Door knob close

27. It is not the 'price' but the 'reasons' for the price that are more important

28. Always have the next step defined

29. To retain the customers

    a. Form a relationship

    b. Be a COLLABORATOR, not a vendor

    c. Ask for feedback – every time

    d. Stay connected – connect at least 6 times in a year

    e. Keep tracking your customer's performance

    f. Ask for reference and endorsement

30. To ensure success, the rule is to PRACTICE – PRACTICE - PRACTICE

Feedback Form

Your feedback is important and is precious! Do fill up this form, click or scan and mail it to **workbook@rajeevnarang.in**

Please score as per your rating between one to five, where 1 is the lowest and 5 is the highest.

1. The overall experience of the Workbook?   – – – – –
2. Usefulness of the Workbook?   – – – – –
3. Content clarity in the Workbook?   – – – – –
4. Use of examples in the Workbook?   – – – – –
5. Engagement of the Workbook?   – – – – –
6. Will you recommend Workbook to others? – – – – –

If you are happy, clap your hands and say a few words of encouragement.

If the workbook didn't fulfill your expectations, share your thoughts and suggestions here. Say a few words of encouragement, for sure. It will help us improve.

_____

_____

_____

_____

_____

Name: Mobile: Email: